Cambridge **Discovery Education**™

▶ **INTERACTIVE READERS**

Series editor: Bob Hastings

ALIENS
IS ANYBODY OUT THERE?

A2

Genevieve Kocienda

CAMBRIDGE
UNIVERSITY PRESS

DISCOVERY
EDUCATION™

CAMBRIDGE
UNIVERSITY PRESS

University Printing House, Cambridge CB2 8BS, United Kingdom

One Liberty Plaza, 20th Floor, New York, NY 10006, USA

477 Williamstown Road, Port Melbourne, VIC 3207, Australia

314–321, 3rd Floor, Plot 3, Splendor Forum, Jasola District Centre, New Delhi – 110025, India

79 Anson Road, #06–04/06, Singapore 079906

Cambridge University Press is part of the University of Cambridge.

It furthers the University's mission by disseminating knowledge in the pursuit of education, learning and research at the highest international levels of excellence.

www.cambridge.org
Information on this title: www.cambridge.org/9781107660007

First published 2014
20 19 18 17 16 15 14 13 12 11 10 9 8 7

Printed in Dubai by Oriental Press

A catalogue record for this publication is available from the British Library.

Library of Congress Cataloguing in Publication data
Kocienda, G.
  Aliens : is anybody out there? / Geneieve Kocienda.
    pages cm. -- (Cambridge discovery interactive readers)
  ISBN 978-1-107-66000-7 (pbk. : alk. paper)
1. Life on other planets--Juvenile literature. 2. English language--Textbooks for foreign speakers.
3. Readers (Elementary) I. Title.

QB54.K53 2013
576.8'39--dc23

                          2013025130

ISBN 978-1-107-66000-7

Additional resources for this publication at www.cambridge.org

Layout services, art direction, book design, and photo research: Q2ABillSMITH GROUP
Editorial services: Hyphen S.A.
Audio production: CityVox, New York
Video production: Q2ABillSMITH GROUP

Contents

Before You Read:
Get Ready!

What do you see when you look up at the sky at night? There is the moon, and there are many, many stars. But is there more? Are there living things? And can we talk to them?

Words to Know

Read the information. Then complete the definitions below with the correct highlighted words.

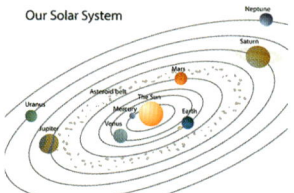

The Sun and the Earth are part of our solar system. It has eight planets.

Some scientists use telescopes to try to answer the question: Are there other living things far from Earth? And if there are, are they intelligent?

People have built spacecraft to travel through space to look for other living things.

1 _____ : smart, can understand and learn
2 _____ : big, round things like Earth
3 _____ : a star, like our Sun, and the planets around it
4 _____ : people who study the natural world
5 _____ : where you find solar systems
6 _____ : special planes that travel far from Earth
7 _____ : machines that make things look bigger

Words to Know

Read the definitions. Then complete the paragraph with the correct words.

aliens: living things that do not live on Earth

astronomers: scientists who study space

communicate: give information to another person

make contact: find out where someone is and communicate with them

search: look somewhere to find something

universe: everything in space: the Earth, moon, stars, Sun, and more

The **1** _____ is very, very big. We don't know everything that is in it. Many people think that there could be living things, or **2** _____ , that live far away from Earth. **3** _____ use telescopes and spacecraft to **4** _____ space for these beings and to let them know we are here on Earth.

Maybe one day we will find intelligent beings – or they will find us! But what will happen if we **5** _____ with them? How could we **6** _____ with them? We don't know their language, and maybe they cannot understand any of the languages of the people on Earth.

CHAPTER 1

Little Green Men

IS THERE INTELLIGENT LIFE BEYOND EARTH? SCIENTISTS ARE TRYING TO FIND OUT.

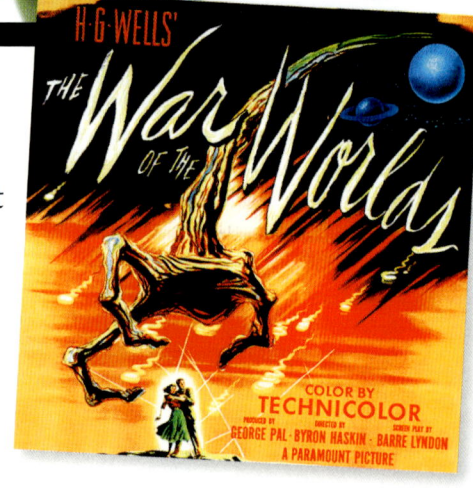

Do you think there are aliens that live on other planets in the universe? What do you think they look like? In science-fiction books and Hollywood movies, the aliens are often "little green men" with long, thin bodies, very large eyes, and hands with only three long fingers. They travel in "**flying saucers**." In some movies, like *E.T. the Extra-Terrestrial*, the alien is very kind and friendly. In other movies, like *The War of the Worlds*, the aliens are dangerous. They want to kill everyone on Earth.

No one knows what aliens really look like – or if they really do exist.[1] However, some scientists think that the universe is so big that intelligent life must exist **beyond** our world.

But scientists are not waiting for aliens to come to Earth in flying saucers. They think that the first contact with aliens will be with messages. So scientists are trying to find messages from aliens – and at the same time, they are sending messages. They hope that their messages can be the beginning of communication with aliens.

The scientific way to say "aliens" is "extraterrestrial intelligence." *Extra* means "out" and *terrestrial* means "of Earth." So *extraterrestrial intelligence* means any intelligent life-form[2] that lives outside of Earth.

Do you think aliens will receive our messages? Will they communicate with us in words or in another way, like musical sounds? That's what the aliens did in the movie *Close Encounters of the Third Kind*.

[1] **exist:** live
[2] **life-form:** any living thing

ANALYZE

Why do some people think that aliens are friendly? Why do others think they are dangerous?

The Arecibo radio telescope has a 305-meter antenna.

CHAPTER 2

SETI

COMMUNICATING WITH EXTRATERRESTRIAL LIFE-FORMS IS NOT JUST SCIENCE FICTION. IT IS REAL SCIENCE.

JODIE FOSTER
MATTHEW McCONAUGHEY

CONTACT

In the 1997 movie *Contact*, a scientist is trying to find proof[3] that extraterrestrial life exists. She uses a special radio to listen for messages. One day, she hears messages from a far away star. The messages tell her how to build a machine that will let her travel to that star.

Does this sound like a strange story? Well, it's based on the work of real people at a real organization[4] that wants to make contact with extraterrestrial life-forms.

[3] **proof:** something that shows that a thing or idea is true

[4] **organization:** a group of people who work together to do something important

It's called the SETI Institute. SETI stands for "**Search** for Extraterrestrial Intelligence." SETI has many important scientists. They are trying to find out if there is life in the universe beyond Earth.

The SETI Institute was started in 1984 in California, USA. But the search for extraterrestrial intelligence started earlier.

In 1960, a young radio astronomer named Frank Drake started the first search for **signals** from other solar systems. He used a 26-meter antenna, but he didn't hear anything. Many other scientists, however, were interested in his **research**.

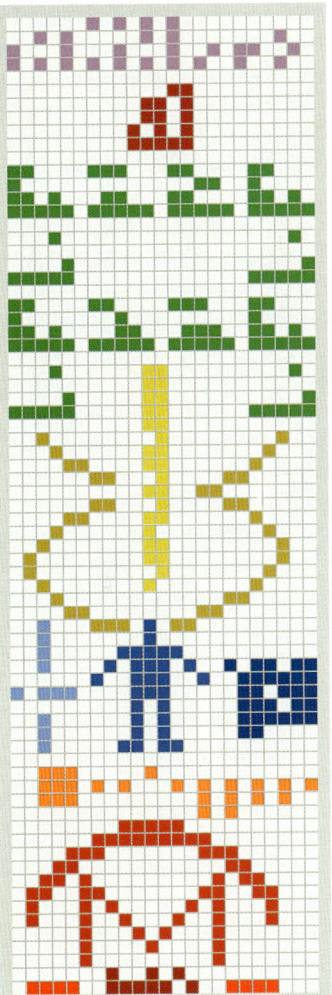

In 1974 the famous Arecibo Message was sent from a 305-meter antenna. It was the strongest message ever sent. The message was a simple picture. Scientists think prime numbers may be easier for aliens to understand, so the picture is 73 lines of 23 characters per line (73 and 23 are prime numbers). The picture shows a person, our solar system, DNA, and some of the chemicals[5] of life.

[5] **chemicals:** things like oxygen, hydrogen, and nitrogen that are needed for life on Earth

The Arecibo Message

Ten years later, a group of scientists started the SETI Institute. Today, SETI does many different kinds of research.

One part of SETI uses radio to listen for messages from other intelligent life-forms. Why radio? People started sending radio signals into **space** about 100 years ago. We do it every time we turn on a radio, a TV, or use radar.[6] So, maybe, other intelligent life-forms send out radio signals, too. Maybe one day we will hear alien radio programs!

The SETI Institute also uses telescopes to look for extraterrestrial intelligence. What do they look for? Short but strong lights that are not natural. They think these lights could show that aliens are trying to send signals to us.

[6] **radar:** radio waves used to look at weather and also far away things

Radio telescopes

Can we live somewhere out there?

Another part of SETI, the Carl Sagan Center, studies astrobiology, which is the study of life in the universe. They want to answer these questions: Where did we come from? Are we alone?

The Carl Sagan Center also researches habitability – if and how people can live in a place. They study different kinds of habitability on Earth, in very difficult places like the Arctic, Antarctica, the highest mountains, and the bottom of the ocean. They also research habitability in other places in our solar system. They want to find out if there are other planets where people could live. To do this, scientists from the National Aeronautics and Space Administration (NASA) fly into space, and they also use the world's best telescopes to look into space.

Video Quest

The SETI Institute

Watch this video to learn more about the search for aliens. What kind of signal does the SETI Institute search for?

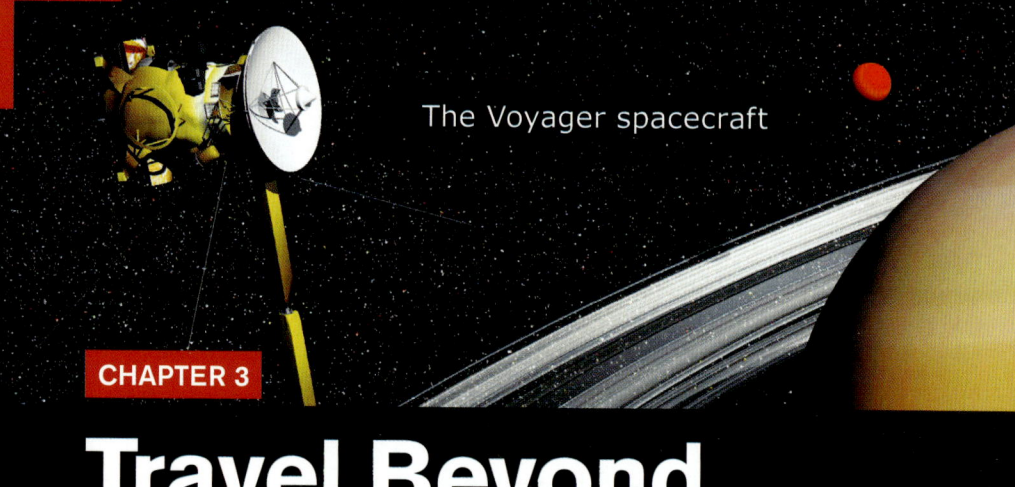

The Voyager spacecraft

CHAPTER 3

Travel Beyond Earth

THE EXPLORATION OF SPACE CONTINUES.

The job of NASA is to research and **explore** space. It was started in 1958. Only eleven years later, in July 1969, Neil Armstrong became the first person to walk on the Moon.

In 1977, NASA sent two spacecraft, Voyager 1 and Voyager 2, on a mission[7] to explore the planets Jupiter and Saturn. These spacecraft are unmanned – they don't have any people on them.

Jupiter and one of its moons, Io

[7]**mission:** a trip to do one special job

They found that Jupiter's moon Io has active volcanoes. They also explored the rings around Saturn and sent information that helps scientists understand them better.

A volcano

After exploring Jupiter and Saturn, however, Voyager 1 and 2 didn't stop. They have sent a lot of information back to Earth. And some of it is very interesting. Here is more information about the Voyager spacecraft:

- In 1989, Voyager sent the first color pictures of the planet Neptune.

- In the beginning, the Voyager spacecraft were going to explore only two planets for five years, but they have already explored all the large outer planets of our solar system and 48 of their moons.

- In 1990 Voyager sent the last pictures of our solar system.

- In 1998 Voyager 1 became the farthest away man-made thing in space.

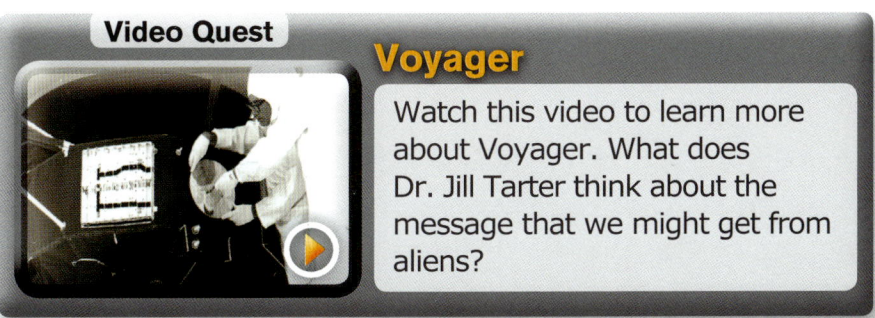

Video Quest

Voyager

Watch this video to learn more about Voyager. What does Dr. Jill Tarter think about the message that we might get from aliens?

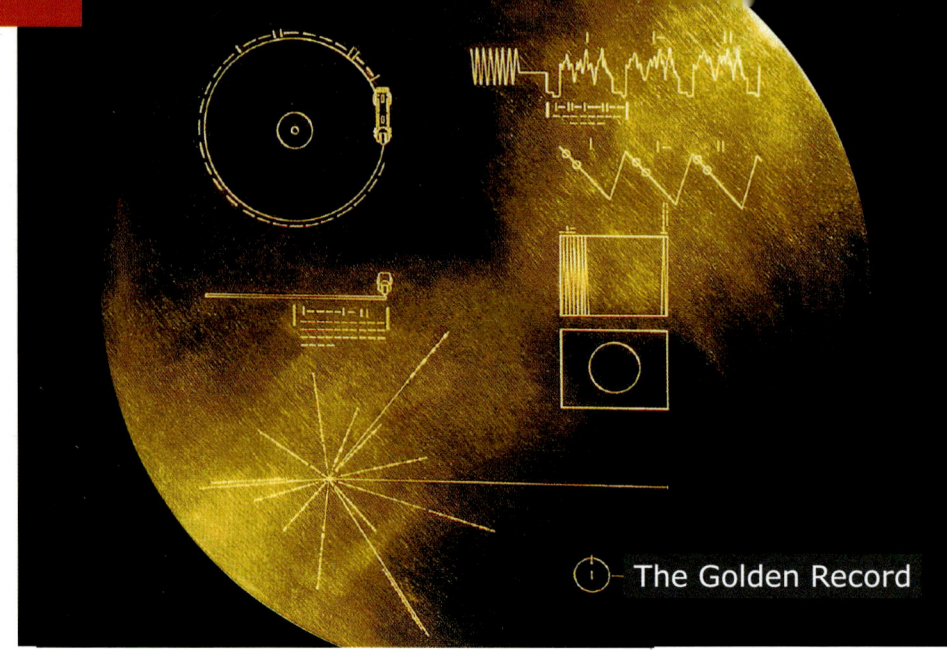

The Golden Record

As of 2014, the Voyager mission is in its 38th year. The spacecraft are now past Pluto and out of the heliosphere – the area around the Sun. They are still sending information back to NASA.

But what about searching for and making contact with extraterrestrial intelligence? That is a part of the Voyager mission, too.

Both Voyager spacecraft have "the Golden Record." It is a greeting[8] to any life-forms that Voyager meets. The message is carried by a 305-millimeter record made of the metals gold and copper. Scientists at NASA chose 115 pictures and many natural sounds including bird songs, wind, and the sea. They put those things on the record to show what life on Earth is like. They also chose music from different countries and times and spoken greetings in 55 different languages.

....

[8]**greeting:** a welcome to someone, like saying "hello"

Of course, the United States isn't the only country to explore space and search for extraterrestrial life.

Russian scientist Konstantin Tsiolkovsky researched building spacecraft as early as 1883. Research in Russia, and then the Soviet Union, continued, and in 1957, Sputnik 1 was the first satellite in space.

Sputnik was the first satellite to go around the Earth.

Yuri Gagarin

The Soviet Union also had the world's first manned space flight. In April 1961, Yuri Gagarin, on the spacecraft Vostok, became the first man to travel in space around planet Earth. It took him 108 minutes.

Today, Russia still has a space program. It is also one of the countries that work on the International Space Station. Maybe by working together we will find out if we are alone or if there is more intelligent life in the universe.

The International Space Station

EVALUATE

Why do you think the scientists wanted to put many different pictures, sounds, and music from different countries on the Golden Record?

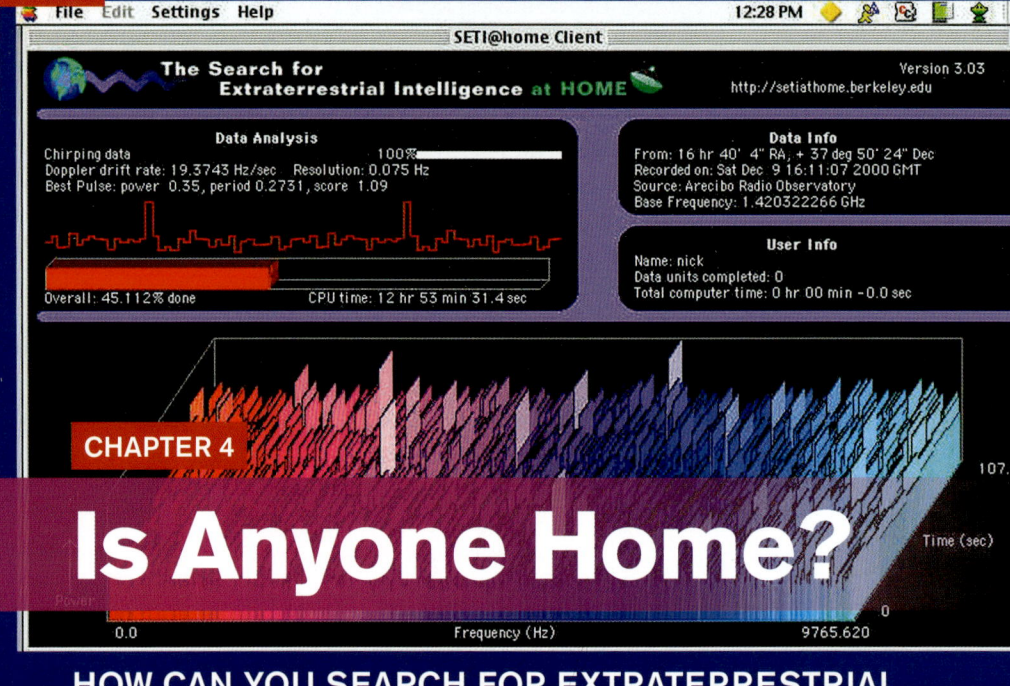

The Search for
Extraterrestrial Intelligence at HOME

Version 3.03
http://setiathome.berkeley.edu

Data Analysis

Chirping data   100%
Doppler drift rate: 19.3743 Hz/sec   Resolution: 0.075 Hz
Best Pulse: power 0.35, period 0.2731, score 1.09

Overall: 45.112% done   CPU time: 12 hr 53 min 31.4 sec

Data Info

From: 16 hr 40' 4" RA, + 37 deg 50' 24" Dec
Recorded on: Sat Dec 9 16:11:07 2000 GMT
Source: Arecibo Radio Observatory
Base Frequency: 1.420322266 GHz

User Info

Name: nick
Data units completed: 0
Total computer time: 0 hr 00 min -0.0 sec

CHAPTER 4

Is Anyone Home?

Power

Time (sec)

107.

0

0.0   Frequency (Hz)   9765.620

HOW CAN YOU SEARCH FOR EXTRATERRESTRIAL INTELLIGENCE WHILE SITTING AT HOME?

SETI wants the search for extraterrestrial intelligence to be open to everyone. So they found a way to help people join in. How? With a program called SETI@home. Here's how it works:

SETI usually uses large computers that study **data** from very big radio telescopes, like the one in Arecibo. But these computers don't have enough power[9] to study all the data that they get from the telescopes. They only study the strongest signals. To study all the signals they get – from the weakest to the strongest – they need a much more powerful (and much more expensive) computer.

[9] **power:** Something that is big and strong has power.

So that's where you come in . . .

The SETI@home project wants to borrow your computer when you aren't using it. How can they borrow your computer? They give you a screen saver. When you are not using your computer, the

SETI@home is a screen saver for your computer.

screen saver gets some data from SETI and puts it on your computer.

Your computer then studies the data and sends the information back to SETI. As soon as you want to use your computer again, the screen saver stops studying the SETI data. Then, when you stop using your computer, the screen saver starts studying the data again.

In this way, SETI@home is made up of many small home computers, all studying different pieces of data at the same time. It's almost like having one very big computer!

Video Quest

Hello?

Watch this video to learn about the SETI@home program. How many people are in the program?

So, with all the scientists, telescopes, radios, and computers, have we made contact with extraterrestrial intelligence? Or have they tried to make contact with us? Maybe.

The Wow Signal

Ohio State University, USA, August 15, 1977

Astronomer Jerry Ehman is looking at some data from a radio telescope called the "Big Ear." Ehman sees a group of numbers and letters that are completely different from anything scientists have seen before. Is it a signal from space? The signal is loud, and it lasts for 72 seconds. Then it stops. Ehman writes "Wow!" next to these numbers and letters.

Scientists looked and looked, but they could never find the same signal again. Was ET trying to call us? Or was it a wrong number?

The Roswell Aliens

Roswell, New Mexico, USA, July 8, 1947

Was the Roswell flying saucer really just a weather balloon?

A flying saucer falls from the sky and crashes on a farm. Inside the spacecraft are some aliens. A newspaper tells the story. But later that day, the army says it wasn't a flying saucer. It was a weather balloon. And there were no aliens.

In 1978, Stanton T. Friedman, a scientist interested in flying saucers and aliens, talks to Jesse Marcel. In 1947, Marcel was a US Army official at Roswell. He says there was an alien spacecraft and that the Army took the aliens to study them. Other people come forward and say that they saw aliens, too. But the Army repeats its story. It was just a weather balloon.

Some people think Roswell shows that aliens exist. But there is no proof.

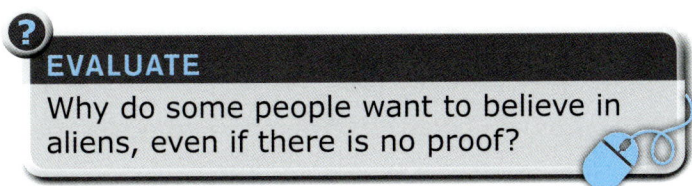

EVALUATE

Why do some people want to believe in aliens, even if there is no proof?

CHAPTER 5

What Do You Think?

PEOPLE HAVE DIFFERENT IDEAS ABOUT ALIEN CONTACT. HOW DO YOU FEEL ABOUT IT?

How do you feel about contact with extraterrestrial life-forms? Do you think we should try to contact aliens? The famous scientist, Stephen Hawking, does not think it's a good idea for us to send messages into space or to answer messages from space. He thinks it might be dangerous for us. Do you agree?

Think about this: You are watching the news on TV. The big story is that scientists have received a message from space. Do you think that's good news or bad news? Why?

Now, read these news stories. How do you feel about each one – excited, worried, afraid, interested, or something else?

1. Scientists at SETI say they got some kind of message from space. It might be an intelligent message, but it might just be electrical signals. They don't know and can't find out. They will have to wait and see if another message comes.

2. Scientists at SETI say they got a message from space. They are sure that it is from an intelligent life-form, but they can't read it. We may never know what the message says.

3. Scientists at SETI say they got a message from space. It is in a mathematical language, so we can read it. The message is:

   Hello, Earth. We are coming to your planet.

After You Read

Read the questions and choose Ⓐ, Ⓑ, or Ⓒ.

1 How do scientists think the first contact with aliens will happen?

   Ⓐ They will send a message.

   Ⓑ They will come to Earth in a flying saucer.

   Ⓒ They will send a satellite.

2 *Extraterrestrial* is another word for what?

   Ⓐ spaceship

   Ⓑ alien

   Ⓒ telescope

3 What is the Arecibo Message?

   Ⓐ a very big telescope

   Ⓑ a simple picture

   Ⓒ a screen saver

4 When did we start sending radio signals into space?

   Ⓐ in 1960

   Ⓑ 100 years ago

   Ⓒ after the first man walked on the Moon

5 What does SETI use telescopes to look for?

   Ⓐ strong lights

   Ⓑ flying saucers

   Ⓒ pictures of aliens

6 What is the Golden Record?

   Ⓐ a telescope

   Ⓑ a spacecraft

   Ⓒ a message

Video

7 What is NOT on the Golden Record?

   Ⓐ photos of war

   Ⓑ Earth's location in space

   Ⓒ sounds of nature

8 What was special about the "Wow Signal"?

(A) The signal happened a few times.

(B) Scientists never saw a signal like this before.

(C) Scientists could understand the signal.

Complete the Text

Use the words in the box to complete the text.

aliens	intelligent	scientists	spacecraft
communicate	planet	solar system	universe

Do you think there is **1** _____ life beyond our

2 _____, the Earth?

Most **3** _____ don't think there can be

4 _____ living in our

5 _____, but maybe there is extraterrestrial life

somewhere in the **6** _____. Maybe one day we

can **7** _____ with these life-forms. And maybe

they will come in a **8** _____ to visit us!

Your Opinion

If aliens come to Earth one day, what do you think they will be like? Think of three ways they will be like us and three ways they will be different.

Like us

_____

_____

_____

Different from us

_____

_____

_____

Answer Key

Words to Know, page 4
1 intelligent **2** planets **3** solar system **4** scientists
5 space **6** spacecraft **7** telescopes

Words to Know, page 5
1 universe **2** aliens **3** Astronomers **4** search
5 make contact **6** communicate

Analyze, page 7 *Answers will vary.*

Video Quest, page 11
One that cannot be produced in nature.

Video Quest, page 13
Just like our message on the Golden Record, they might put only the good things about themselves.

Evaluate, page 15 *Answers will vary.*

Video Quest, page 17
Eight million

Evaluate, page 19 *Answers will vary.*

Choose the Correct Answers, page 22
1 A **2** B **3** B **4** B **5** A **6** C **7** A **8** B

Complete the Text, page 23
1 intelligent **2** planet **3** scientists **4** aliens
5 solar system **6** universe **7** communicate
8 spacecraft

Your Opinion, page 23 *Answers will vary.*